Time and Other Things That Fly

Jane Calender Christison

Copyright © 2020 by Jane Calender Christison

All rights reserved.

No part of this book may be used or reproduced in any manner whatsoever including Internet usage, without written permission of the author.

ISBN#: 978-1-7347392-0-6

Library of Congress Control Number: 2020905351

Poetry and original artwork by Jane Calender Christison

Design by Deborah Perdue, Illumination Graphics

*To my family
and, as always,
to my husband, Ken*

I never think of the future.
It comes soon enough.

Albert Einstein

CONTENTS

Persistent 2

The Silence Between 5

Cocktail Hour with a Red Hummingbird 6

Flying, a Further Thought 8

Business Question 10

I Am Not Sure How This Happened 11

Moon Fantasy 12

The Thief 14

Morning Glories 17

A Thought to Ponder 18

A Message 20

Stinging Bee 23

Cloud Sweeping 24

Inches in the Stream of Time 26

To the Beach Parade 28

The Turning Plan 30

White Note Interlude 32

Laundry 33

The Spirit Rain 35

Perpetual Wings 37

The Dove Tree's Secret 38

Sandpiper Story 40

Timing 41

Question 42

A Fight with Aging 44

Imagine This Joy 45

Half Full 46

Brief Appearance 49

Owl Visit 50

Beethoven Without a Scowl 52

No Regrets 53

Ode to Autumn 54

Time, a Work in Progress 56

Of Dimensions 59

A Book in One Sentence 60

A Short Life of Poppies 62

A Thank You Note 63

Fantasy of the Clock 64

How to Find More Time 66

This Is Not a New Thought 68

Acknowledgments 71

About the Author 73

FROM THE AUTHOR

There never seems to be enough time, and what little time there is goes faster and faster. One day we awaken to find *later* is here. Like most young people, I figured time was unlimited and rarely thought about the later shortage. Now I hear the persistent voice of Maurice Chevalier in the movie *Gigi*, when he sings about youth: "I remember it well!"

I also ponder the words of Augustine, a fourth-century Christian bishop, who, when asked by a parishioner, "What is time?" answered, "What we measure not, is not." Somehow, I have ended up with a group of poems about time. And birds flew into many of the poems! Birds are often the subject of my drawings and paintings, so the illustrations are a natural fit for this book.

Even without an urgent need to think about the years going by, I hope some readers might identify with my thoughts, which can touch a nerve at any age, for through the years most of us encounter the subject of time and other things that fly.

Persistent

Time does not interest a raven,
ruffle a butterfly or a honey bee,
concern a robin or a river
and certainly not an ocean
forever busy with complex matters.

But I dream of stopping time —
without dying, of course.
How do I do that?
I hold my breath,
but that will kill me faster.

I return to breathing —
I concentrate on *slow*,
focus on a thought:
in between my breaths, time is not passing —
will I live longer (if not forever)
if I slow my breath and stretch time?

What if I pray harder?

What if I live faster,
move faster,
speed up everything I do,
and fit more living into the minutes,
so it will seem as if I have
more of them left to use?

But what if I land
on a different hill of my mind
and see I am the temporary
shelter of a soul
not measured by time,
a soul which always was
and always shall be?

The Silence Between

One way to quiet a restless mind is
to find the silence not silent,
    wisdom written long ago,

to picture the great blue heron,
slow-stepping,
making no sound,
no ripple on the still water
    in the chapel of reeds,

to hear peace,
music not in the notes,
but in between the notes,
music sweeter than the little songbird
    could ever sing.

Prophets heard Spirit
sing in the silence not silent,
    and told of it.

Cocktail Hour with a Red Hummingbird

Twilight, a time for miracles —

out of the red-topped tree by our balcony
shot a red-headed hummingbird,
the first red one ever to visit our garden.

Announcing himself with a whir,
he dove by our bistro table
into the tall purple lavender
to hang in the air,
sip his own fragrant cocktail,
and share with us the red sunset sky,

until like a ruby spark,
he spun around
and dove back into the red-topped tree.

But he did not take the memory with him.

Flying, a Further Thought

I know I can fly —
I could start as a sparrow in a nest
of twigs and paper and string,
or as an egret in a treetop nest
of sticks and plants,
or as a hummingbird in a tiny nest
bound with spider silk
woven onto a slender branch.
I would grow stronger every day,
until I could leave the nest and fly free.

However —
I suppose in my current life
I am not in truth a bird,
but if I believe I can fly,
the perfect love that blesses my days
will, at the right time,
give me the wings I need.

Business Question

If you have ever considered borrowing time,
where would you go to borrow it?
Is there a shop somewhere in town
or in some office on the second floor
of a building close by?

What would you need to use as collateral?
And where could you get
more time, not borrowed, not stolen,
to pay back the loan?

Have you thought about the result?
If you *were* able to borrow time,
there might be a reckoning later —
would you chance entering a Faustian land?

And what if you had used up
all the borrowed time
and realized there was no more to be found?
The safest answer is not to borrow it
and to fill every second of life to the brim
with *thank you!*

I Am Not Sure How This Happened

It was not my choice to get older,
to see the years go by too fast,
but I guess there is no reverse
in this auto's gear shift.

I still want to run up hills and stairs
and dance all night
like the beautiful young people
who will find out soon enough
what it is like
to be thought of
as a relic,
a Model T Ford,
a paper book with pages to turn,
or a product of
the dark ages of last week.

I did not choose to have
so many years in back of me
when I would like them in front,
but the overall plan
was drawn up long ago,
and since I cannot
change the sequence,
I can learn to go deeper . . .
into the moment,
into quiet thought,
into no time.

Moon Fantasy

In the time of quiet,
imagine you can
fly into your
moon mind,
a mind within a mind,
uncharted time
when you live
on the moon,
love on the moon,
dwell on a secret part
of the moon —
a beautiful land
where you are light
and can pull
sheets of that light
over the dark
places of the earth.
You can always go
into the time of quiet
and imagine flying
into your moon mind
for the light.

The Thief

It is easy to guess
who the feathered thief is —
he is the one who steals music
from other winged performers,
mixes up the notes
to create his own compositions
and performs on telephone wires,
branches, rooftops,
whatever spot suits his fancy.
You can walk near this little
cluster of feathers,
and he doesn't fly off —
he is eager
to sing his songs to you,
to show off his talent for improvising
and to share his happiness.
You have guessed right;
this shoplifter
is a song sparrow!

Morning Glories

All summer long,
in the reeds
of the mudflats,
blackbirds
with wings on fire
sing out in absolute joy.

I think they sing to the One
who collects rainwater
to fill blue vessels of glory
that wind over
old wood fences
along the marsh.

The birds drink from the cups
and trust that God,
with His seasons of rain,
will watch over the flowers
and the red-wings.

A Thought to Ponder

This year, or years from now,
I may awaken one morning
and realize
that God has given me
eternal life —

I will know this without question.

The thought
is not alarming,
until the next question:
am I living eternal life right now?

No one has said I am not!

A Message

Through a winter drizzle,
along the freeway lanes I drove,
in a hurry like the other drivers
for important reasons,
reasons not important if I were
on another planet hanging in space,

but I was on earth,
and life on earth can find reasons
for anything.

As the winter day darkened,
I wondered why
a cluster of white feathers
was floating over the traffic ahead —
no, the feathers were not floating at all;
they were attached
to the wings of a snowy egret,

a white message
of beauty and peace
flying above the insane rush below.

Stinging Bee

It stings, a little dagger of death,
the honey bee
in a beautiful garden.
No one taught this small winged demon
what happens to it after it stings.

I know God does listen and soften
the fear and the sting of my thought,
but the clock, ticking away
in this lush flower garden,
repeats "limited time, limited time."

I cherish mornings
and evenings
and the time between them,
and the words "I love you" —
I will block off the vision
of a chasm ahead,
and stop and treasure
precious minutes
and words of love —
I want nothing else.

I need to cast away fear,
and leave the bee to revel
in the sweetest flowers,
a bee forever content, alive,
fulfilled and not called to sting.

Cloud Sweeping

Imagine there are hands holding
white cloud feathers
like brooms to sweep the sky
ahead of the black monster clouds
peering over the hilltops,
cloud creatures creeping up
to pour water all over the earth below.

Birds know that when the time is right,
the hands will bring out
bulky white cloud brooms
to sweep away the dark monsters
and open the blue again.

Imagine you can sweep away
a worry with a cloud broom.

Inches in the Stream of Time

Have you ever thought about
measuring time in inches
to make life seem longer,
or measuring the years
in crocuses and tulips,
black sweet plums,
slow peeling bark,
or in autumn dust,
which would take forever?

You could put winter
into another box of thought
and think of living an inch at a time,
measuring a wide, intense blue sky in inches
or black cloud billows blown up with rain.
Could you measure the wind in inches?

Listen to the music of Mahler,
who did not analyze
how much more time he had,
did not concern himself
with the black rain clouds,
or with the dark wings of his world,
but wrote sunlight
and power and brilliance
and grace notes of love into his music,
without wasting time
worrying about more years,

or about tossing
inches of days and music
that did not measure up
into the wastebasket.

To the Beach Parade

You at two or ten or twenty
will never quite believe,
that the *you* of you
will be the same *you*,
at fifty, or one hundred three,

the same *you* with your
pail and shovel,
soccer ball, or doll,
in slouchy pants,
in four-inch sandals,
the *you* is still the same in all.

The *you*, running down a hill to first love,
or burning with the thrill of life,
the *you*, holding your forever love,
your star of earth and sky,

is the same *you* slowing on a stair,
the *you* that could run fast,
the *you* ambitious in your prime,
now dreaming of the past,
of pesky pimples on prom day,
of a perfect body in salty surf —
that body now is less than perfect;
today to truth it must defer.

And now that you're
not two or twenty —
you're nearer to one hundred three,
you'll say to that familiar *you*,
"Why did I never see?"

For when you look out from your perch
on mountaintop or somewhere under,
whether toddler, teen, or now antique,
you are the same miraculous wonder.

The Turning Plan

Ask a curlew, ask a plover
or ask the tiny sanderlings, legs racing
in a blur of sticks.
It is no use to ask a seashell —
for no one is at home.

Ask God. He will give you
a most simple answer,
"In the beginning . . ."

Surf, sand, shells, wood and seaweed
turn and turn in the world of the beach,
where salt and sun sculpt
driftwood and bones,
and toss them about the sand.

Any one of us could end up
as a random shape,
a sculpture, to be smoothed and polished,
turning with sand and tides,
turned by God and sea and wind
with the bones, seaweed ropes,
shells and starfish washed with soft colors,
and cast onto other beaches
to turn and turn
in perfect harmony.

Ask God.
"In the beginning . . ."

White Note Interlude

Somewhere in the deep
of your past,
on a sandy beach,
you watched
a group of white seagulls,
each with its
own steady monologue
punctuated with
shrieks —
dissonance instead of the
harmony you were searching for
beside the waves,

until without warning,
a full wave of gulls
flew off screeching,
leaving a beach
with a quiet surf,
the white music of the Lord,
notes of calm
that dwell in the pauses
of the orchestra
of life's periodic
shrieking days.

Laundry

Could rain
ever wash clean
the untidiness
of the world?

Could the sun
bleach the dirt,
the evil,
the problems woven
into the global cloth?

Could the pristine results
be neatly folded

and put in perfect order
in a universal
linen closet,

to be tended
through all time
by the rain and the sun

and the Hand that folds?

The Spirit Rain

No sound falls —
not on the roof, the skylights,
not on the river rocks
lining the path
to our front stairway.

Like castles on a wine glass,
water castles streak the windows,
slant over the dark form
of the laurels outside,

and deep in the leaves
where cobwebs glisten
as the weaver works silently,
rain washes and polishes
the feathers of a nighthawk.

Time is wearing slippers.

Rain prayers are falling,
silent prayers that dwell
in the pauses of storms.

Perpetual Wings

Love is busy,
a bumble bee
in the summer
blooming
by our window.

Wings graze through
tastes, scents and silk,
in the lavender, rose and
jasmine sweetness to satisfy
simple hunger and thirst,
nectar always ready
for the untroubled bee —
a lesson for you and me,

for love is busy
spreading its wonder
over the fields of our days.

The Dove Tree's Secret

It is not a secret —
the celebration outside our kitchen windows
where dense leaves rustle and almost hide
a frantic flapping of wings.

I will be polite
and stay busy with other things.
But I will know when the leaves are still,
and I will watch the shadow of a wing
emerge from the dark,
cross over the tall grass and disappear
in the branches of a tree across the hill.

Two doves, each now in a separate tree,
call and answer,
the sound plaintive to some ears,
but not to the doves
connecting with the musical memory
of their morning in the Love Tree.

Sandpiper Story

Stepping
on the sky
in the mirror
of water
spread
across the sand,
brittle-legged
sandpipers
scroll over
a Genesis tale
of light
and life
repeating.

Timing

Whenever I think
I wish my love and I
had met sooner,
I realize
I must thank God that
we met at all
and that He knew
the best timing,
the only timing possible.

As we did for so many years,
we could have
again
walked right by each other —
this time numbed
by our separate darkness —

and never said hello
and never known
the blessing of us.

Question

What do you advise,
O sage, O wise one?
I see time running out for me.

The sage answers:
Let the thought go.

Leave behind you
the obsession about time passing,
and think only of the minute
you are in right now.

Go even deeper into that minute —
go into its timeless space.

The love around you will intensify
with the reality of its power.

A Fight with Aging

I shall wear a big hat, fitted jeans,
shoes with medium heels — not too high,
or I might trip and fall.

I shall wear green nail polish, or blue,
use the latest beauty products in a jar,
wear quiet jewelry, no sparkles.

I have figured it out:
I shall move by people so fast
they cannot see me!

I shall hike for miles,
do yoga, stretch,
and drink lots of water,

lift weights to get stronger
so I can fight and win
battles with the years.

I will smile a lot,
stay out of the hot sun,

and find beautiful
new colors in the shade!

Imagine This Joy

In its charmed life,
a creek doesn't have
to remember
the way
down the mountain —
it takes its music
and falls
down a wooded canyon
over rocks
and small cliffs
in a clear crystal line,
drops into a blue pool
of sky and infinity,
spills over
within a time directed
and continues on,
unhurried,
a creek
of water bells
ringing
down the hill
to meet
creeks of other canyons
and to flow into
the symphony
orchestra of the sea.

Half Full

I do not like the thought of being old,
so I am now practicing
to forget the chronology
and focus on the energy, joy, love,
sparks and songs of the days,

and since math was never
my favorite subject,
I can manage to ignore the numbers
and put some of the years
under a pile of newspapers,
papers that tell me
my years are not the issue anyway —

I haven't finished the music,
the poetry, or the paintings,
or the books I hunger to read.
One of them, the Bible,
tells me I am not old.

And what about loving?
Love gives you wings.
Love expands days and breath and beauty.

I have decided to place the years
deep in the leaves of a lemon tree
on our balcony —
baby lemons are forming in the blossoms.
I can grow with them
and not be old for the nearest tomorrow —

and there may be more tomorrows
coming up than I think!

As I live more years,
I will look back and say
how young I was today!

Brief Appearance

What vagrant thought or breeze
brought the picture of a flat hour?
I was not looking for
the final flat note of a heartbeat,
or for a memoir of that moment
written onto flat waves,
the writing paper of the wind —
I forgot the wind can change in an instant.

The vagrant thought
must go off with the blue seagull.
I will start a new manuscript
without a flat line,
change the picture,
paint a winged shape
that my brush chooses —
maybe the wind has an idea —
and no flat thought needs to enter
the space and beauty of this hour.

Owl Visit

It might have been a block of wood,
the odd, motionless, hunched shape
on the railing just outside my window.
How could I have missed it before —
I walked through the room every day?

The form was not wood at all —
it was a visitor; it was an owl sleeping.
I moved closer —
he looked at me once with his owl eyes,
then closed them.
He must have decided I was no threat;
he was not worried about me
on the other side of the window glass.

I guess the corner of the eaves
seemed safe enough for this morning visitor,
exhausted after his night of gluttony
in the high grass of the hill behind our house —
what misery he left back on that hill,
but after all, he is an owl.

Sometime later,
after dark, he left for another railing
or another hill for hunting,
and every day I still look for him.

Beethoven Without a Scowl

Into a crater of black silence he fell.
How did he send his magnificent,
impossible symphonies flying from
that silence,
notes like powerful horses with manes
streaming
along with his own wild hair?

Out of the nightmare,
out of the frightening, noisy quiet
in his head,
came choral music to be sung to the glory
of the One
whom he might have called cruel.
He made the word *Pathétique* beautiful,
wrote sonatas of power, joy, storm
and sadness,
but never music with a scream.

Doomed to be a recluse, a deaf genius,
his light forever shining,
he dwelt alone with his *Appassionata*
and the miracle of music he heard
flying from his soul.

No Regrets

This afternoon
a striped sparrow
perches on his favorite
tall one-legged
barstool
of dried yarrow

and finds that the bright
yellow of the yarrow field
has faded,
and the seeds
are falling
to the earth,

yet he tarries
on his yarrow top —
he still sees
the colors
of yesterday
and is content
with his moment.

Ode to Autumn

O contrary lady,
stalling, teasing,
you keep one foot with its
glamorous high-heeled shoe
in summer,
the other foot
on the edge of fall.
You postpone winter —
those heavy coats and bulky boots
are so unflattering.

Children, ball players
and fishermen love you
and your warm days,
so you choose to bask in the spotlight
and ignore withered wildflowers,
parched hills
and dried-up streams.

You make the rains wait —
they knock on your door.
You lock it —
you are busy putting
on lipstick and makeup
for your last brilliant show
of gold, orange and crimson
on the fields and mountains

and paths by the rivers.
You persuade the wind
to delay shaking the trees,
but despite your hope,
leaves turn brown
on the branches
and dim your light.

O stubborn autumn,
you stall,
still showing off
your stylish shoes,
colorful clothes
and perfect countenance —
for beauty is your joy —
you want to shine
and delay the inevitable steps of time.
But no more the star,
you are about to be a memory.

You must start your task
of darkening the afternoons early,
and at last, pulling rain,
you begin moving toward winter,
as the late stragglers
of the winged world
stream in long lines through
your now pale persona,
the end of your power to stall.

Time, a Work in Progress

So far, I have not done it —
I have not slowed time down;
in fact, time is speeding up,
a freight train of days flying
with no destination.

Each spring, I watch another tulip bulb
grow an inch a day in my little vase.
You will tell me I have written,
"Measure time in inches."

But time is its own master.

Have you noticed
it was Monday a few minutes ago,
and now the calendar says Friday?
If I stare hard
at the minute hand of my watch,
it speeds up.

Night through the window —
I close my eyes for a second,
and open them to find I am in a new season;
the brightest star has moved
thousands of miles,
and Orion has disappeared
around the corner of the roof.

Day through the window —
the clouds are flying across the sky,
and the wind doesn't listen
to my plea to slow them down.

The only defense is
to erase the fear of time flying —

before fear tarnishes the starlight.

Of Dimensions

We will
never be
never,
not
in this
love
of ours
where
eternal
light *is,*
where sea
and sky
and spirit
are one.

A Book in One Sentence

By now you know
lessons at the school of the sea
come with no pen
to go back and write changes,
no backspace key to see
the same wave breaking
or the same gull flying,

just as lessons at the school of life
teach that an hour lived
is an hour finished —
except for the memory —
again with no rewriting,

but since life and the sea
continue with discoveries of truth,
you can underline
the important words
as you read.

A Short Life of Poppies

On breezy days
when papery
giant red poppies
      bend their
      floppy ears
into the wind,
whole flowers fly off their stems,

and before I can
      question them,
they're gone —
      they drifted away
           so fast —
and soon they are dust,
not even red dust.

If I see them again anywhere,

I will be quick with
my question.

A Thank You Note

How in the world
did God let me live this long?
I am here, alive and blessed!
So many people in my life
left the earth early,
and I am still here nestled in the days.

I am not a Saint Teresa,
or anyone extraordinary,
so how did I receive
the gift of living to this point
and the gift of love every day,
love from those who God somehow
decided to plant in the garden of my life?
I thank Him through all my waking hours
and stand in astonishment.

Fantasy of the Clock

I still find myself wondering
if I could discover a secret cord
to stop time like I can stop it
by unplugging the cord
of my electric clock —
absurd thought —

and even if I could
disconnect time
for a minute, an hour, a day,
I fear that could lull me
into false comfort
and would backfire.

Besides —
I do not think
stopping time
is in God's plan.

How to Find More Time

Sit down in a chair, just sit there —
time will crawl.
Do not fall asleep —
if you sleep,
time will sprint,
and you will run out of it faster.

Fill a large vase with mist —
this is a forever task —
it takes time to find mist.
And even more time to gather it.

Look out your window —
watch each sway of a birch tree
against the sky.
Choose a day when the air is still.
Keep watching for any slight movement —
time won't move.

Watch the space
between blades of grass
on a windy hill —
the space does not move,
only the grass — fascinating.

Go to a field before sunrise —
wait for the orange poppies to open.
If clouds arrive early and stay, you will have
hundreds of extra minutes while you wait.

Stand on a mountain all day
and count the trees,
the blades of grass, the wildflowers.
Look for butterflies and count them.
Stand there all night and count the stars.

And imagine traveling
beyond those stars into infinity
where time does not live.

This Is Not a New Thought

God gave us a little bird
to hold gently in our hands,
to gaze at with amazement,
to feel the pulse,
the wisp of breath,
the miracle.

God gave us
a little bird — *life* —
to hold with great care.

ACKNOWLEDGMENTS

Again I thank Mary Calvez for her editing skills, her patience and her guidance along the steps to publication.

I also thank my book designer, Deborah Perdue, for her creative talent. Always upbeat and positive, she is wonderful to work with.

The support and encouragement of my husband, Ken, keeps me going.

ABOUT THE AUTHOR

*J*ane Calender Christison is the author and illustrator of two other books:

In the Company of Tears, a poetic narrative of the power of love, hope and faith in dealing with grief.

The Sea at the Edge of Light, a book of the healing peace of nature, which she wrote during the years she and her husband lived on the Mendocino Coast.

Her oil paintings are included in *Art of Northern California*. Her watercolors and oils are in many private and corporate collections throughout the United States.

She and her husband live in Marin County, California.

www.ingramcontent.com/pod-product-compliance
Lightning Source LLC
Chambersburg PA
CBHW042119100526
44587CB00025B/4123